My First Maths

What Shape Is It?

Jackie Walter

Notes for practitioners and parents

This series takes a fun, first look at maths in the environment around us.

What Shape Is It? encourages children to recognise shapes by looking at objects found around them.

Challenge children to look around and see how many shapes they can spot - from clocks to windows, sandwiches to sweets.

You could also start exploring 3D shapes. Try sorting 3D shapes into sets using building blocks for example.

Let the children engage with the shapes and ask them lots of questions. Are the surfaces flat or curved? Do they roll?

Do they stack or not? What would each shape be good for? Could you build with it? Could it move easily?

Collect boxes, cardboard tubes and other old packaging. Discuss the shapes and try building models with it,

for example a house, car or robot. Which shapes would be good for wheels, eyes, roof etc.?

Please note, we use the word "corners" in this book but you might also want to introduce the word "angles".

Franklin Watts
First published in Great Britain in 2016 by The Watts Publishing Group

Copyright © The Watts Publishing Group 2016

Credits
Series Editor: Jackie Hamley
Series Designer: Katie Bennett, Kreative Kupboard
Picture researcher: Diana Morris
Consultant: Kelvin Simms
Photo credits:
Svetlana Bayanova/Shutterstock: 3tl, 9b.
Ruth Black/Shutterstock: 5br.
Stefano Carnevali/Shutterstock: 5tr.
Eak/Shutterstock: 2tl, 5cr.
hans engbers/Shutterstock: 18, 24br.
exopixel/Shutterstock: 21l.
Gam1983/Shutterstock: 8tl, 8br.
Gjermund/Shutterstock: 12b, 24tc.
gourmetphotography/Shutterstock: 4br.
irin-k/Shutterstock: 3bc, 22.
Anton Ivanov/Shutterstock: 20c.
Laborant/Shutterstock: 12t, 24tr.
Tuomas Lehtinen /Shutterstock: 15.
lissart/istockphoto: 7.
Veronika Mannova/Shutterstock: 13.
Francesco Messuri/Shutterstock: 5tl.
Mmaxer/Shutterstock: 16.
M. Unal Ozmen/Shutterstock: 3tr, 21c.
RAYphotographer/Shutterstock: 8tr, 8bl.
Eddie J Rodriquez/Shutterstock: 10, 24bl.
Irina Rogova/Shutterstock: 17.

Elena Schweitzer/Shutterstock: 4t.
Eugene Sergeev/Shutterstock: 11, 24bc.
skyhyun/Shutterstock: 5bl.
Somchai Som/Shutterstock: 14, 24tl.
Sopelkin/Shutterstock: 20tr, 21cl, 21br.
StudioSmart/Shutterstock: front cover, 1, 23.
Svitlana-ua/Shutterstock: 2bl, 5cl.
Tobik/Shutterstock: 3bt, 9t.
TOMO/Shutterstock: 6.
Vilor/Shutterstock: 2cr, 4bl.
Sutichak Yachiangkham/Shutterstock: 19.

Disclaimer.

Every attempt has been made to clear copyright.
Should there be any inadvertent omission please apply to the publisher
for rectification.

Dewey number 516.1'5
ISBN 978 1 4451 4926 4

Printed in China

MIX
Paper from
responsible sources
FSC® C104740
FSC
www.fsc.org

Franklin Watts
An imprint of Hachette Children's Group, Part of The Watts Publishing
Group
Carmelite House, 50 Victoria Embankment, London EC4Y 0DZ
An Hachette UK Company
www.hachette.co.uk   www.franklinwatts.co.uk

Contents

Shapes are Everywhere

We see different shapes all around us.
How many different shapes can you name on this page?

ITALIA 800

50° ANNIVERSARIO COSTITUZIONE
CONSIGLIO D'EUROPA € 0,41
ROMA - I.P.Z.S. - 1999
M.C. PERRINI

Flat and Curved Surfaces

Some shapes have curved surfaces like these marbles.

Some have flat surfaces like the wooden blocks.
The surface of a shape is called the "face".

Curved and Straight Edges

Some shapes have curved edges, some have straight edges.

And some have both.

Rectangles and Squares

A rectangle has four corners
and four straight sides.

A square is a special rectangle where all the sides are the same length.

Cuboids and Cubes

A cuboid has six faces which are all rectangles.
A cube has six faces which are all squares
and all the same size.

Cuboids and cubes are good for building.
They fit together without leaving any gaps.

Circles and Ovals

A circle has a curved edge and no corners.
It is flat and perfectly round.

An oval also has a curved edge and no corners.
It is flat, but it is not perfectly round.

Spheres

A ball has a curved surface and it is perfectly round.
This shape is called a sphere. It is not flat.

Spheres are not good for building.
When you fit them together, they leave lots of gaps.

Triangles

A triangle has three sides and three corners.

Look how many triangles you can see on this crane.

Pyramids, Cylinders and Cones

The faces of a pyramid are triangles. It has four faces. The bottom of this pyramid is a square.

This shape is a cylinder.
Its faces are curved and it has
circles at the top and bottom.

This cone has a circle at the
top for the ice cream to sit on.
Its faces are curved and it has
a point at the bottom.

Pentagons and Hexagons

A pentagon is a shape with five sides.
What colour are the pentagons on this football?

A hexagon has six sides. Bees keep their honey in cells shaped like hexagons.

Word Bank

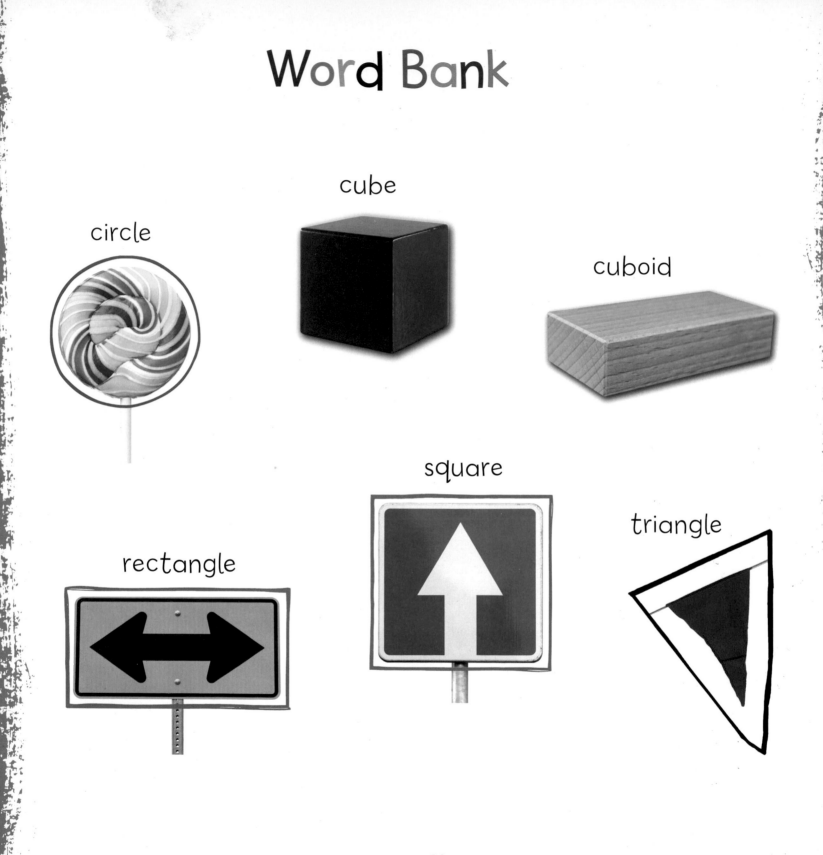

circle

cube

cuboid

rectangle

square

triangle